The Peace Ring

Rosemary Hayes

Illustrated by Ian Newsham

CAMBRIDGE
UNIVERSITY PRESS

Ben and Tracey were moving house. They were taking
things into Ben's new bedroom.

Ben noticed a hole in the wall and pushed his
finger into it.

The hole got bigger and then Ben saw something shining inside. "Hey, Tracey," he said, "come and look!"

Tracey looked. She saw a beautiful ring, shining in its own light. It was stuck inside the wall.

As the children stared at the ring, the hole in the wall grew bigger and bigger. Ben climbed through it and Tracey scrambled after him. It was very dark on the other side.

Ben tugged at the ring, but he couldn't get it out.

"Here, let me have a go," said Tracey. She pulled and pulled and, at last, the ring came free. Tracey held it up. "It's fantastic," she said.

She waved her hand about and, as she did so, rays of light shot through the dark.

"It must be worth a fortune," said Ben. "We'd better tell Mum and Dad."

The children turned to climb out of the hole, but the hole had gone! There was no wall, no bedroom, and no light except the light from the ring.

"What's happened?" said Ben. "Where are we?" His words were lost in the darkness.

Tracey put the ring on her finger and used it like a torch. Dimly, in its light, they could see the

ground beneath them and huge, twisted roots around them.

Ben peered into the darkness and sniffed. "Ugh!
It smells all damp and earthy," he said.

Tracey sniffed too. "It *is* earthy," she said as she
touched one of the roots. "I think we must be a long
way below ground."

"I don't like it in here," said Ben. "Let's get out!"

They looked for a way out. They walked for a long time, ducking and twisting through the roots until they were quite lost.

Suddenly, Ben stopped. "Listen!" he said.

Very faintly, in the distance, Tracey and Ben heard the sound of someone singing in a strange, clinky voice. "It's coming from over there," said Tracey. She shone the ring in the direction of the noise.

"Look!" said Ben. "There's a wall with a door in it!" The children stumbled towards the door, tripping over the roots in their hurry.

When they reached the door, Ben knocked. The singing stopped immediately. Then they heard footsteps and the door opened a crack, sending a shaft of light into the gloom.

"Who is it?" asked a clinky voice. "Who has come to the Earthling Door?"

"Please let us in," said Tracey. "We're lost."

Very slowly, the door opened and a strange girl
looked out. She wore a shiny suit and a bright red sash.
"Earthlings!" she cried. "What has brought you to
my door?"

"Well . . . " began Ben, but then the ring on Tracey's finger sent out a strong ray of light and the strange girl gasped.

"The Peace Ring," she said. "You've brought back the Peace Ring. I knew it would happen one day."

"You did?" said Tracey, looking puzzled.

The strange girl pulled them into a shiny room. "Let me explain," she said in her clinky voice. "My name is Tallic and I am the leader of the people who live down here in the roots. We are called the root-dwellers.

"Up above, in the branches of the trees, live the tree-dwellers. They are led by my brother, Frond – you can see him on the screen. When we had the Peace Ring, we lived in peace. Its light makes everyone happy, you see.

"But one day, the Peace Ring disappeared. Frond said we'd stolen it. Of course we hadn't, but the tree-dwellers didn't believe us. Ever since then we have been fighting. Frond has said that we will never see the sky again until the Peace Ring is returned."

"That's not fair," said Ben.

Tracey smiled and said, "So now you can return the Peace Ring and everyone will be happy again." She began to take the ring off her finger, but Tallic stopped her.

"No," said Tallic. "You two earthlings must return it to us both. If Frond sees *you* with the ring, then he'll know that *I* couldn't have stolen it."

Before Tracey or Ben could reply, Tallic shouted at
the top of her voice, "COME QUICKLY, EVERYONE.
THE PEACE RING HAS BEEN RETURNED!"

Ben and Tracey trembled. Tallic's shout sounded like
a hundred saucepans clattering to the floor.

Suddenly, people were coming from every direction.
They were all dressed like Tallic and they were all

talking at once. The noise was deafening. It was as if all the cymbals in the world were clashing together. Tracey put her hands over her ears.

"QUIET!" shouted Tallic. "We're going above ground!"

The root-dwellers looked frightened, but none of them dared to disobey Tallic.

Tallic took one of Ben's hands and one of Tracey's hands
and led them through twisting passages, up steep steps and
through a metal doorway. The rest of the root-dwellers
shuffled behind them.

They all came out into a large clearing surrounded by huge trees.

"Look!" said Ben, pointing up at the rows of neat tree-houses. "The tree-dwellers really do live in trees!"

There was a rustle in the trees and the tree-dwellers
started to appear. Then the rustle grew into a roar as the
tree-dwellers saw Tallic and the children and the crowds
of root-dwellers.

"To war!" boomed the tree-dwellers. "Fight the
root-dwellers! Force them back underground where they
belong."

The root-dwellers looked scared. They were blinking
in the strong sunlight and edging back towards the
metal door.

Then Tallic stepped forward. "Frond!" she shouted. "Come down from the trees. The Peace Ring has been returned!"

When they heard this, the tree-dwellers went quiet.

"It's a trick!" someone said.

"Show us the ring!" someone else shouted.

Tallic grabbed Tracey's hand and held it up. The sun
flashed on the ring and sent back rays of fire. There was
a gasp of wonder from the tree-dwellers, and then another
gasp as a young man swung down from the branches and
landed at Tallic's feet. He looked very angry.

"So you have decided to give it back at last, Tallic?" said the young man. "About time, too!"

"We didn't take it," said Tallic.

"Of course you did!" shouted Frond.

The other tree-dwellers started to close in on Tallic.

Ben cleared his throat. "She's telling the truth," he said. "My sister and I found the ring and it led us to Tallic."

"It's true," said Tracey.

For the first time, Frond looked at Tracey and Ben. He stared. "You are earthlings!" he said.

Quickly, Tallic turned to Ben and Tracey. "Both of you hold the ring," she said quietly, "and then hand it to both of us."

"What will happen?" whispered Tracey.

"I don't know," said Tallic. "Just hold tightly to my sash and then hand us the ring."

Slowly, Tracey eased the ring from her finger. Then she and Ben held tightly to Tallic's sash as they handed over the ring.

As soon as they let go of the ring, Ben and Tracey felt themselves being lifted up into the air. They were still holding on to Tallic's sash, but she was on the ground.

For a minute they drifted in the air, looking down on the tree-dwellers and the root-dwellers.

Tallic and Frond were standing together, their arms
around each other. All the tree-dwellers and the root-
dwellers were getting together, too, shaking hands,
laughing, and hugging each other.

Then Tallic and Frond looked up and waved to Ben
and Tracey.

At that moment, a strong force dragged Ben and Tracey back, back through the metal door, back through the Earthling Door, back underground, back through the tree roots, on and on, hurtling back so fast they could see nothing at all.

With a crash, they burst through the wall into Ben's new bedroom and landed with a thump on the floor. They sat up. The hole in the wall had closed up. But between them lay a shiny, red sash.